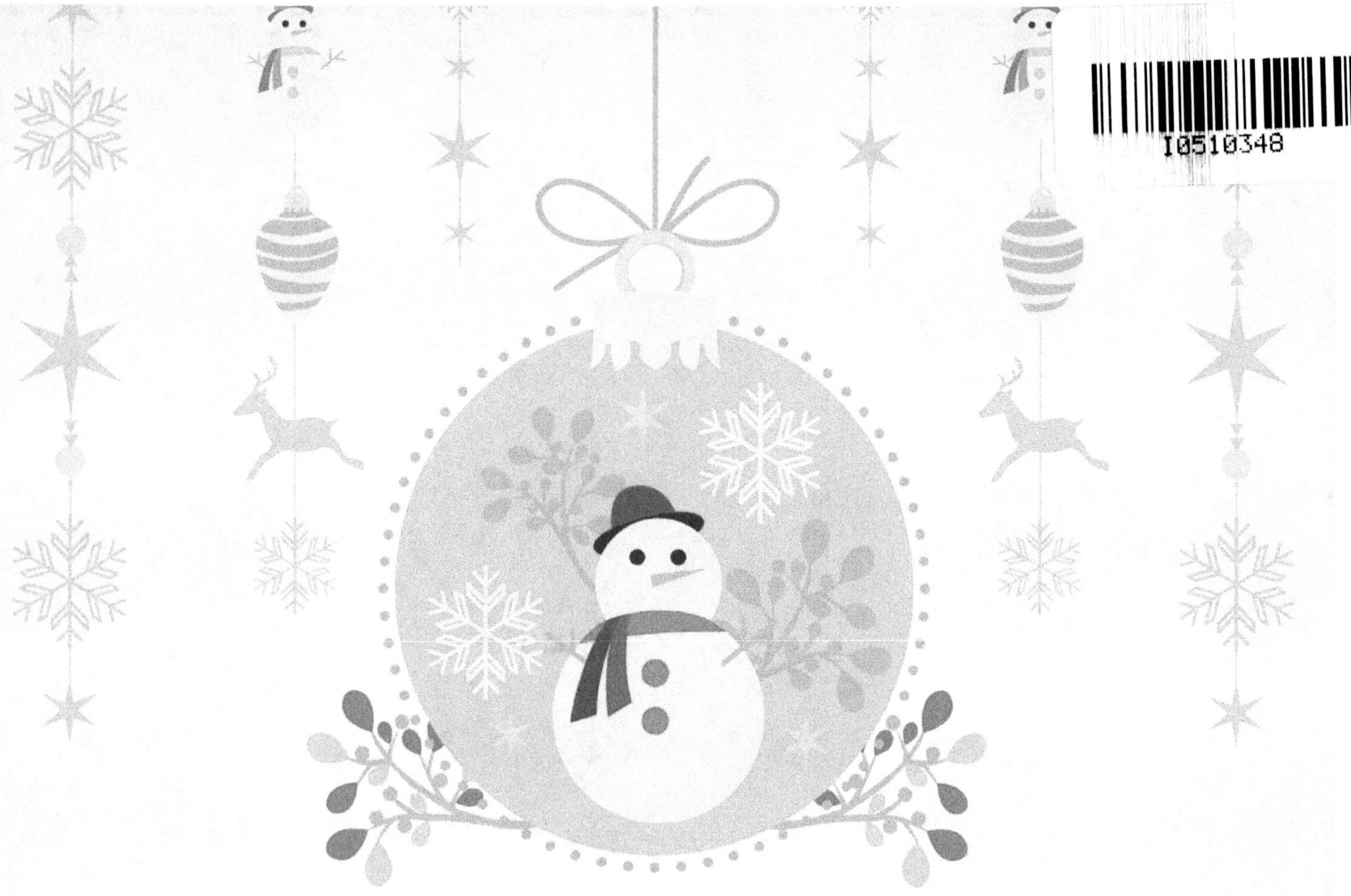

Merry
CHRISTMAS

This Books Belongs To

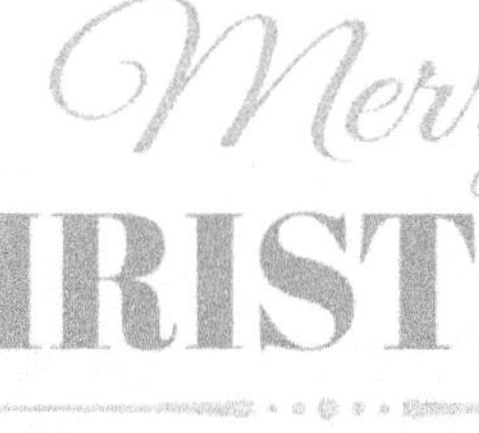

....

....

....

....

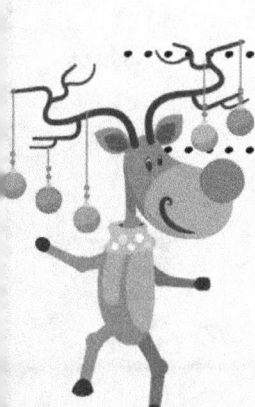
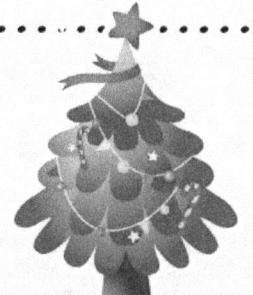
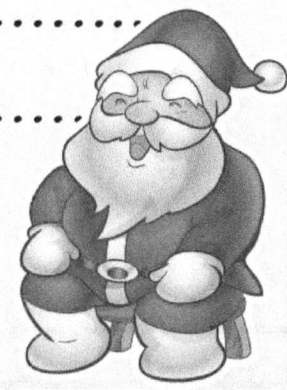

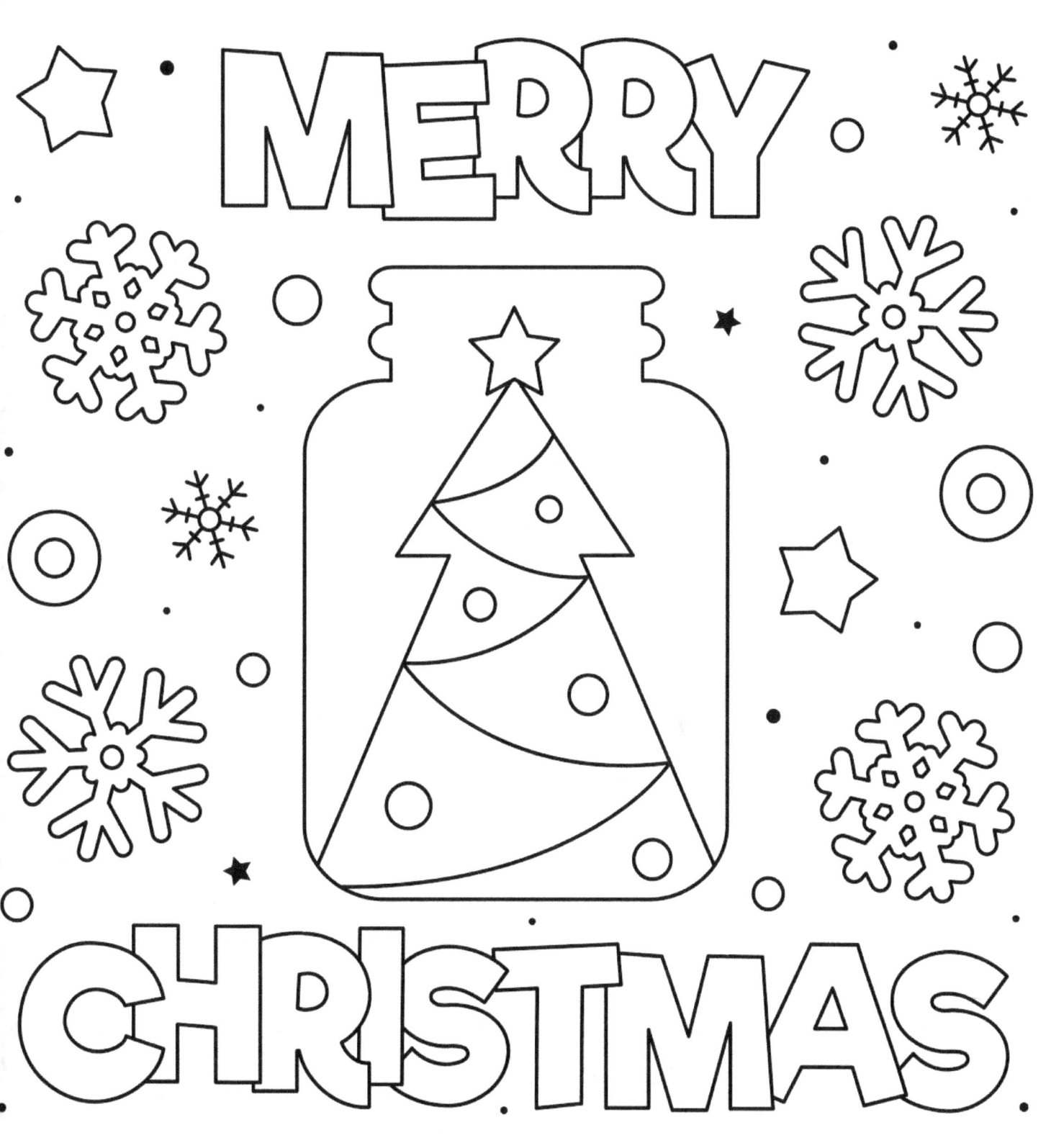

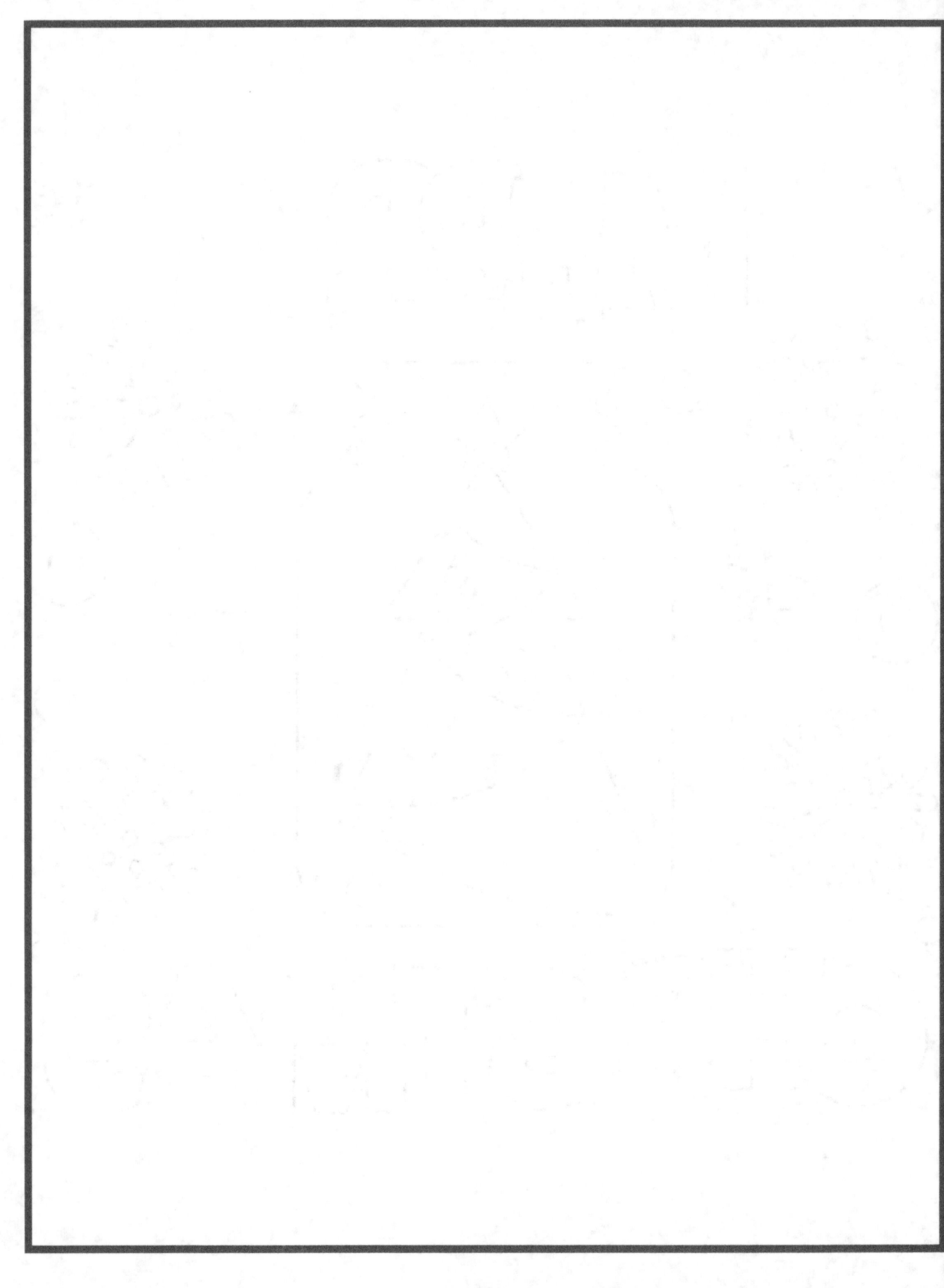

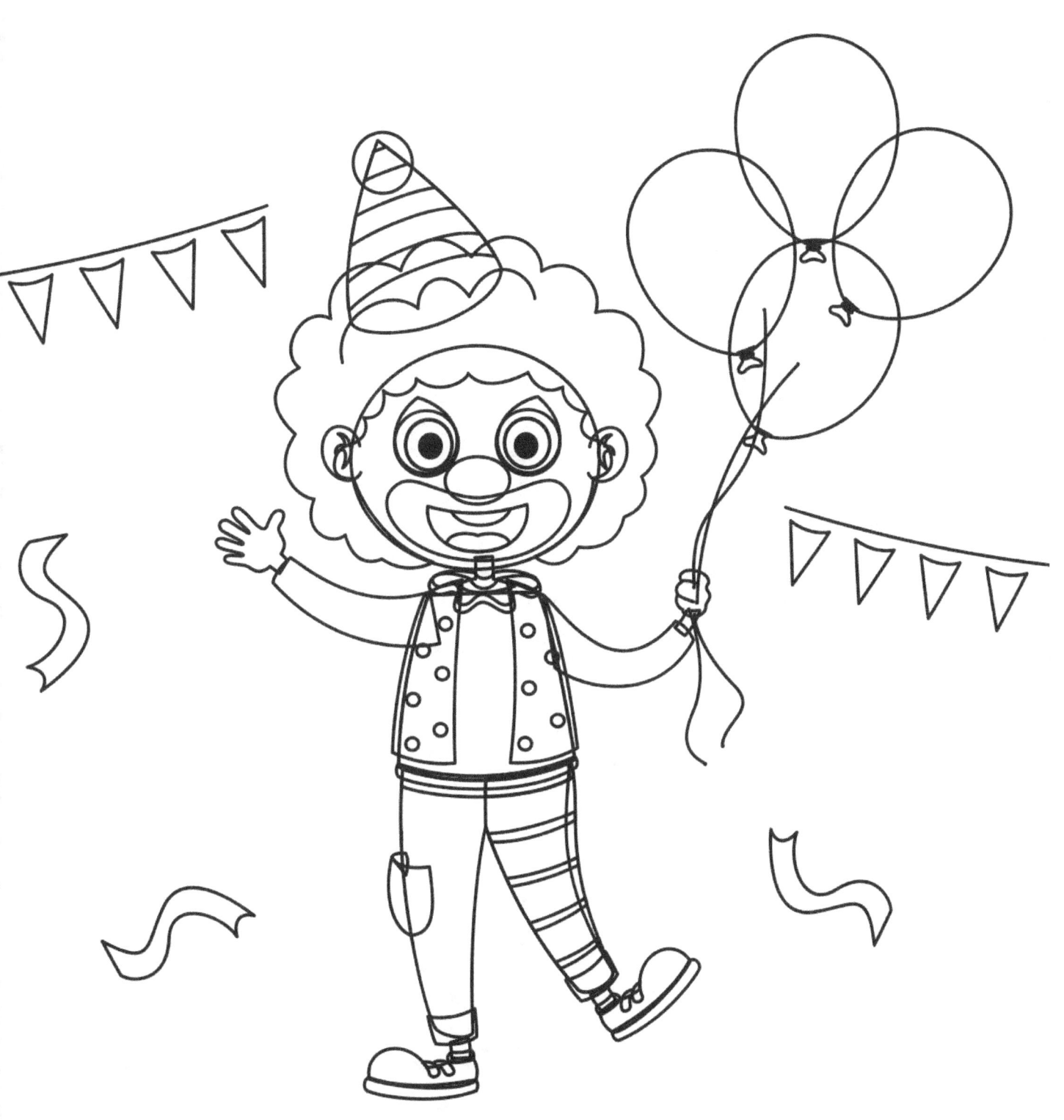

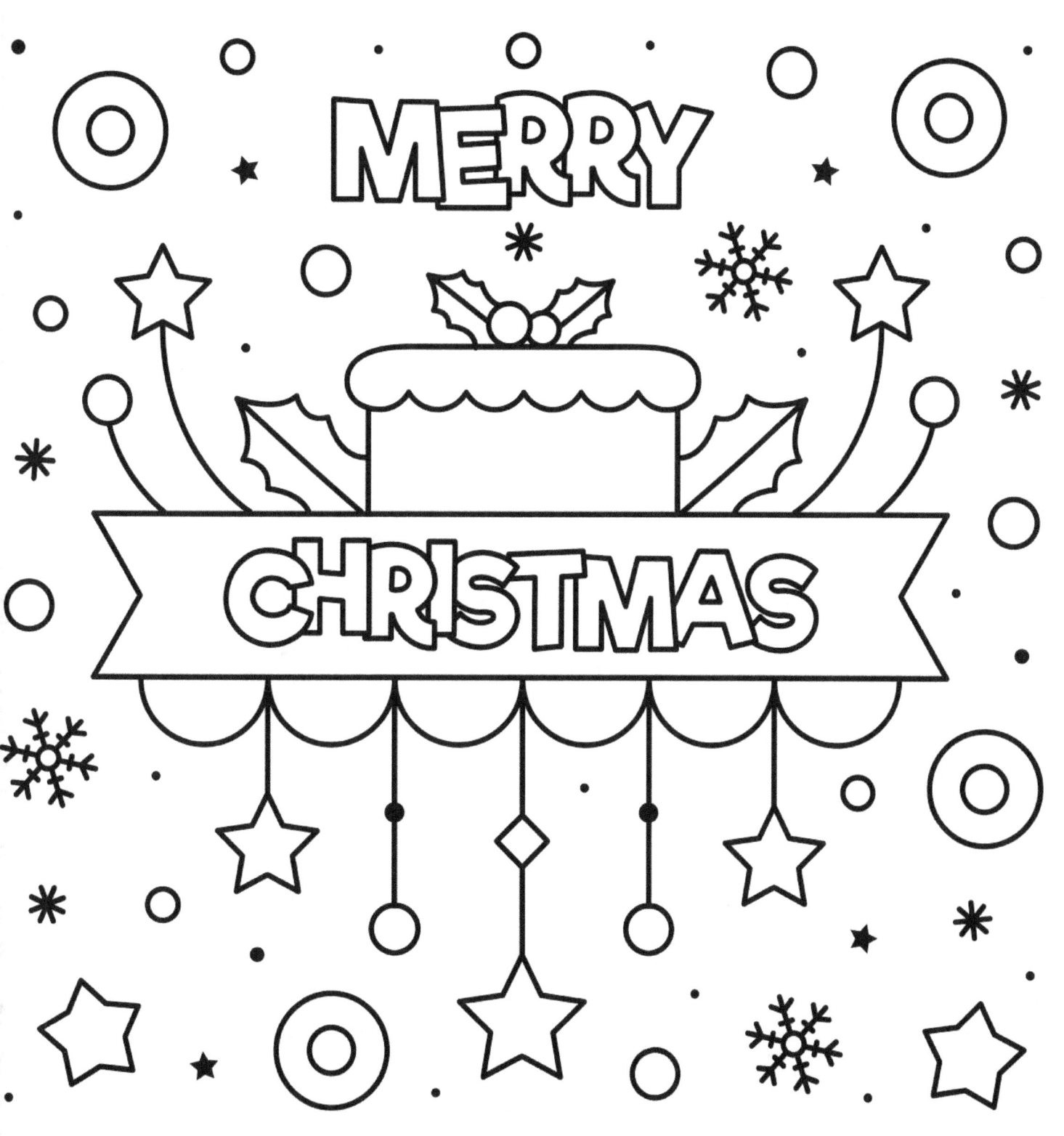

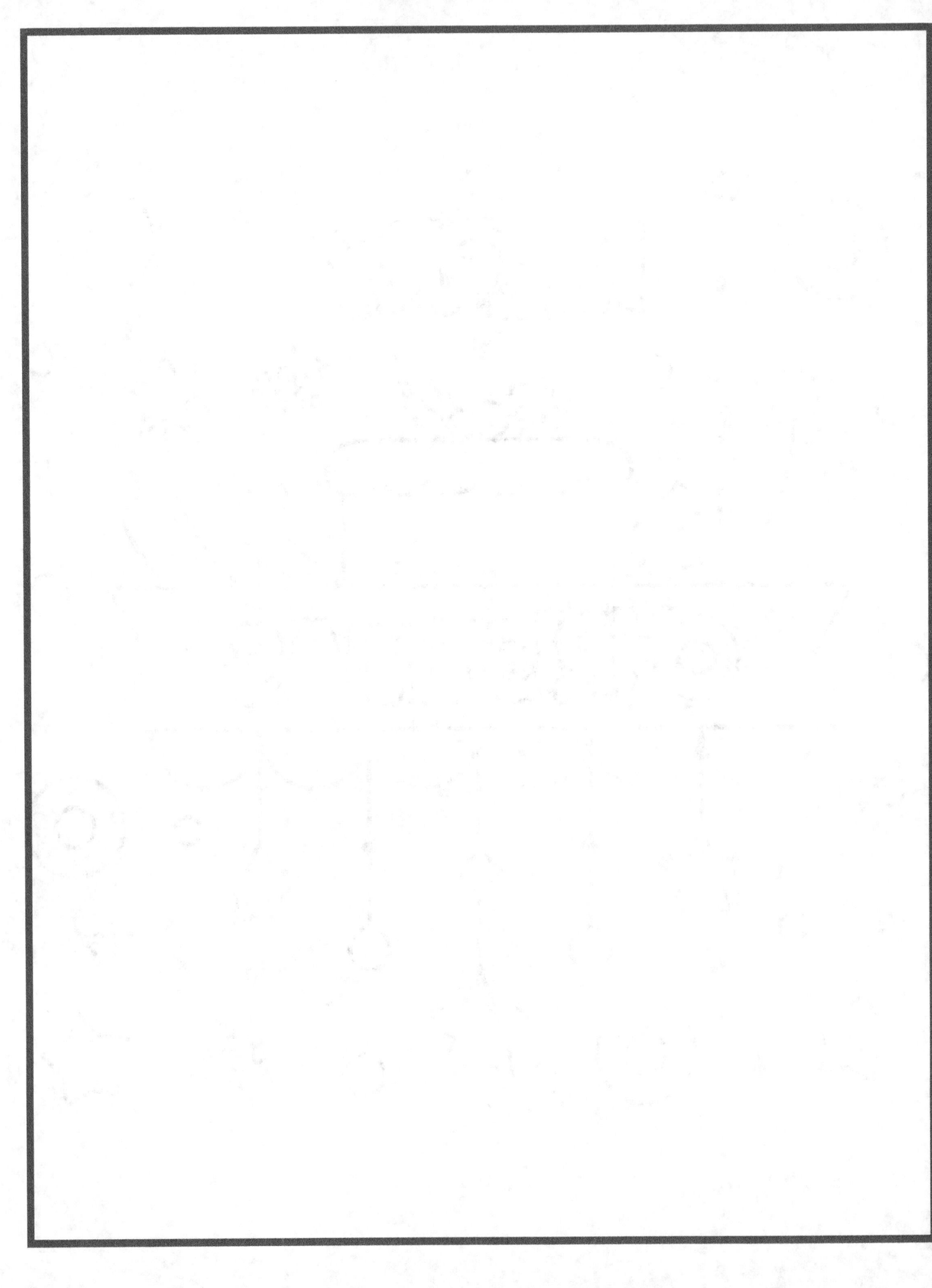

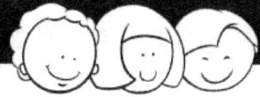

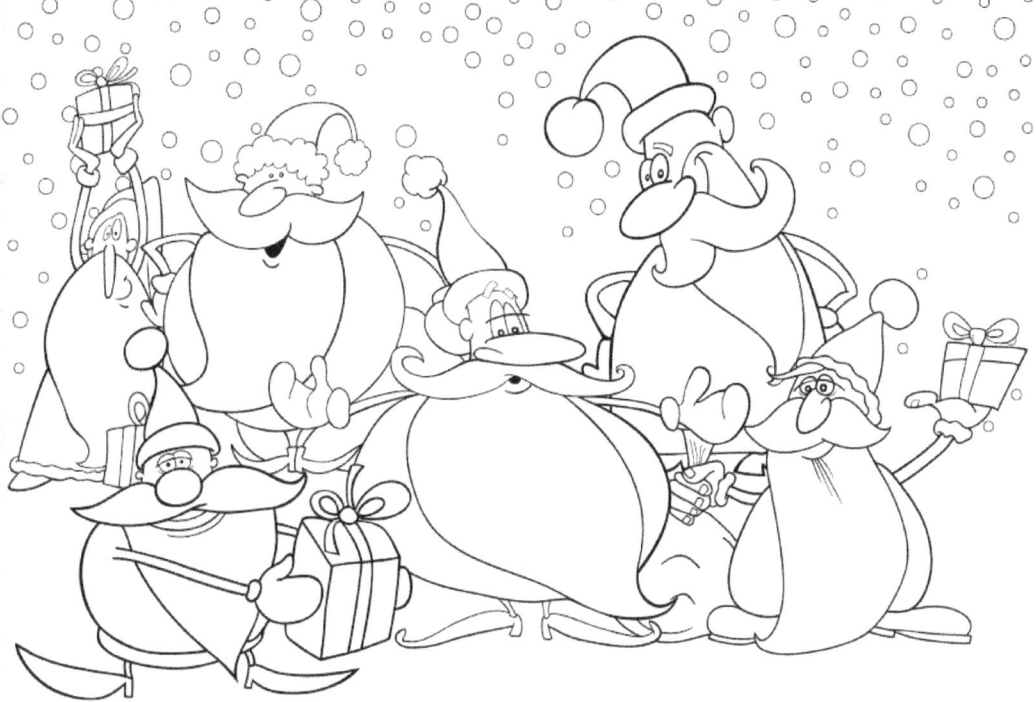

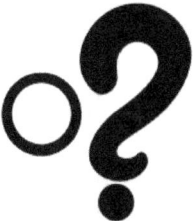

FIND
7
DIFFERENCES

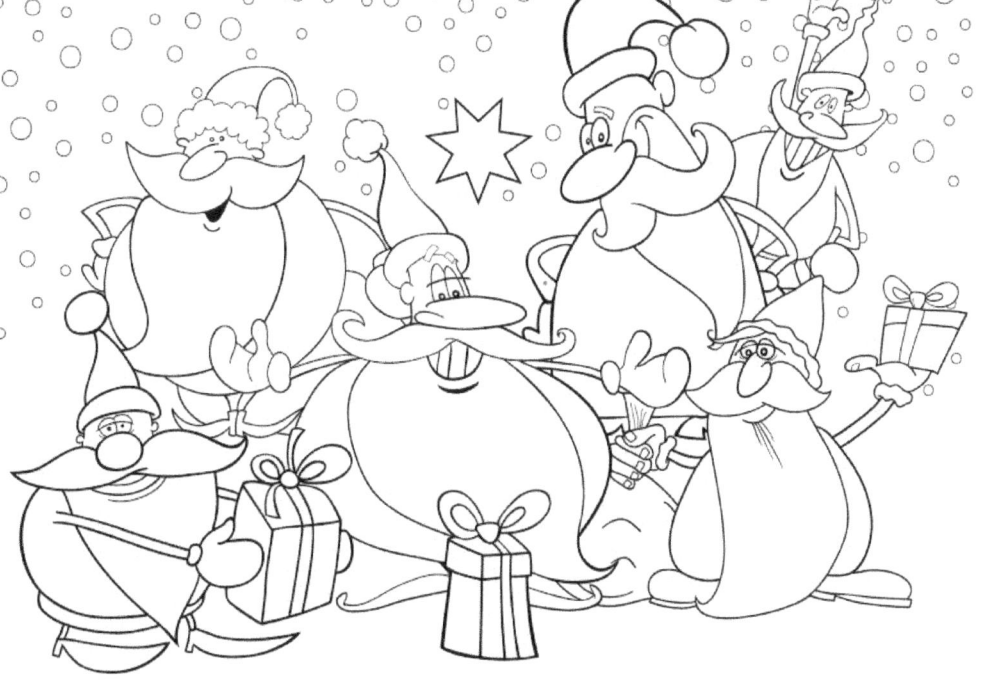

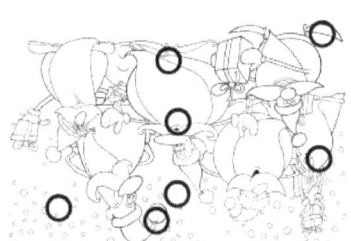

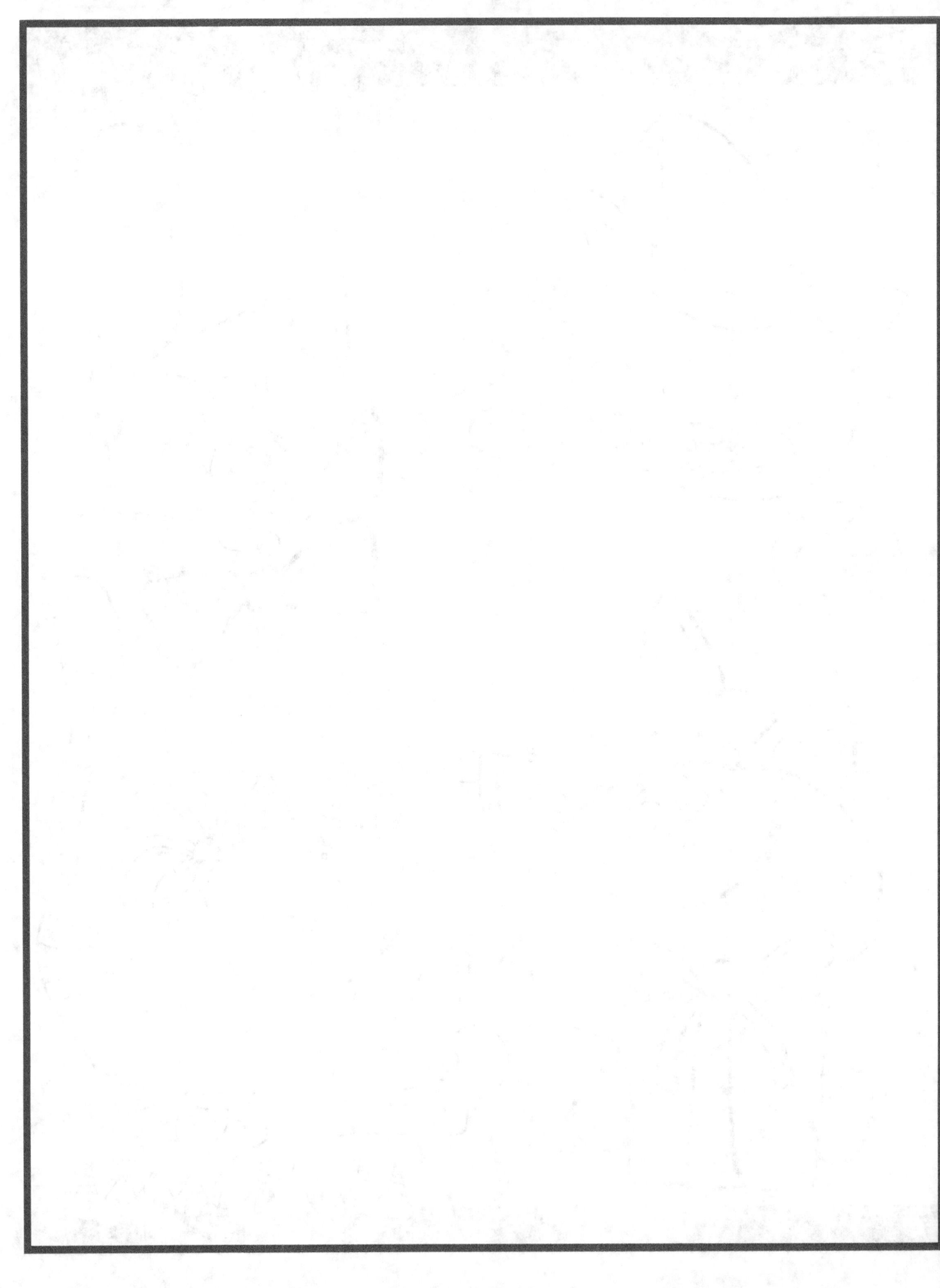

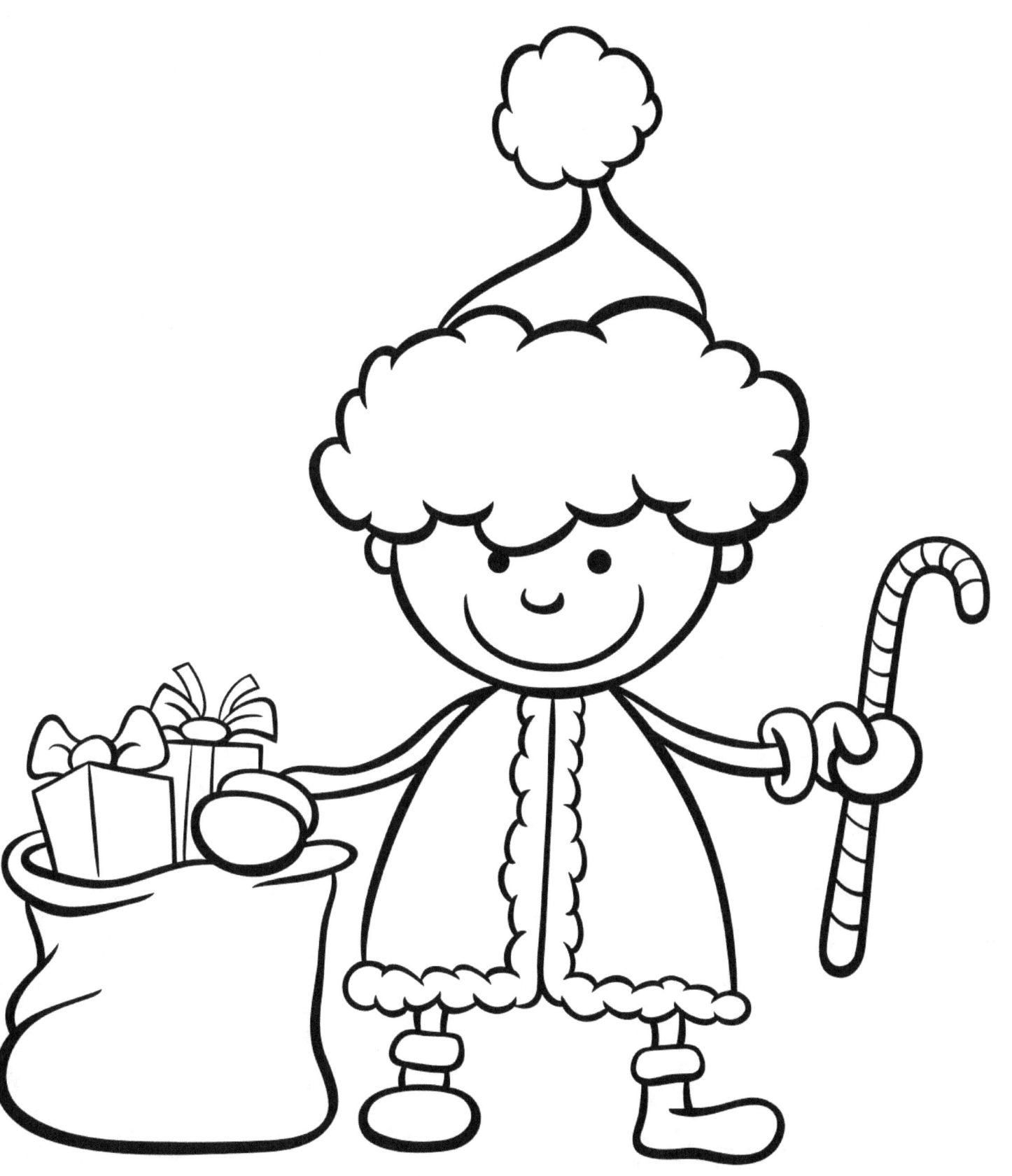

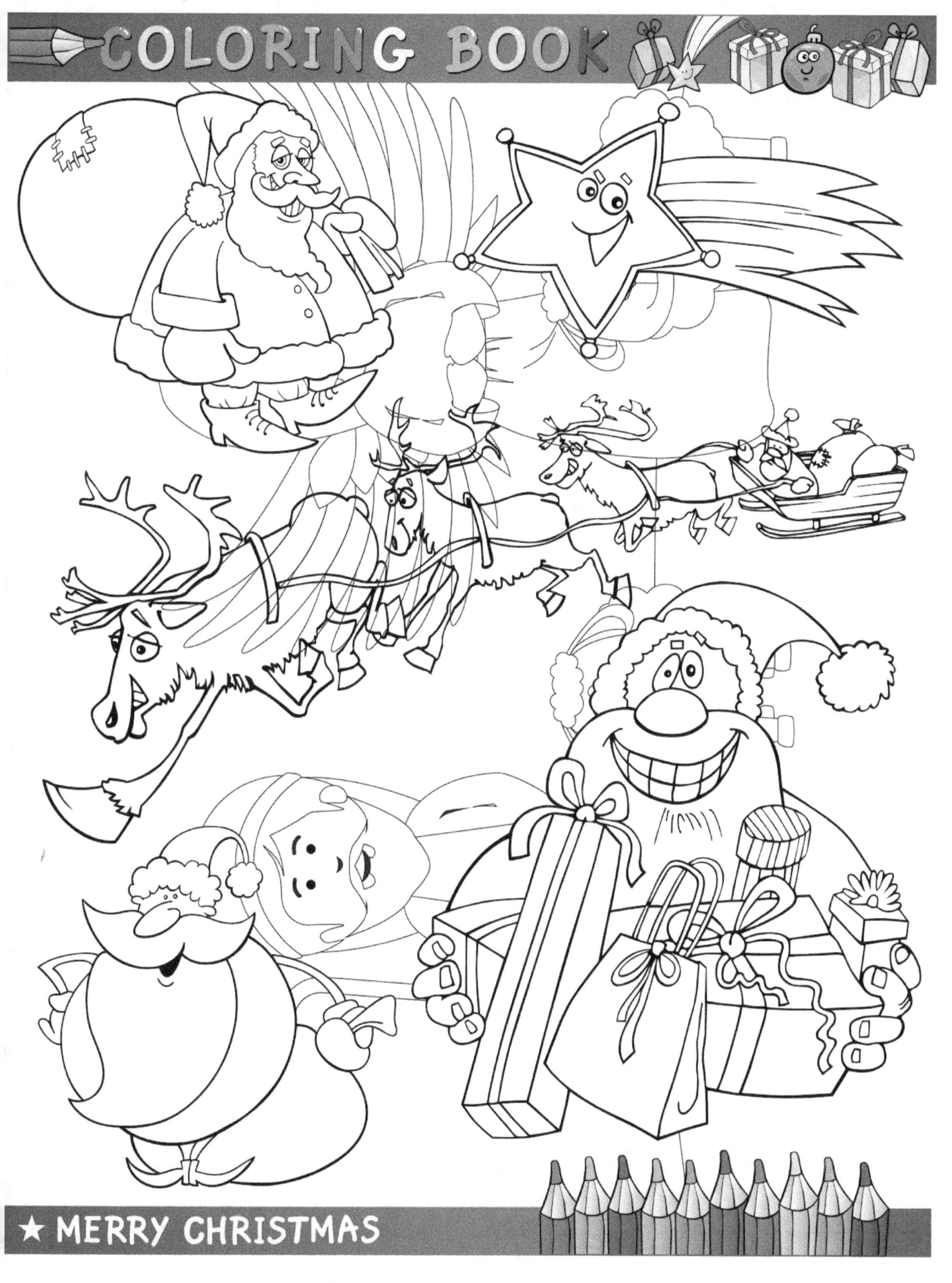

COLORING BOOK

★ MERRY CHRISTMAS

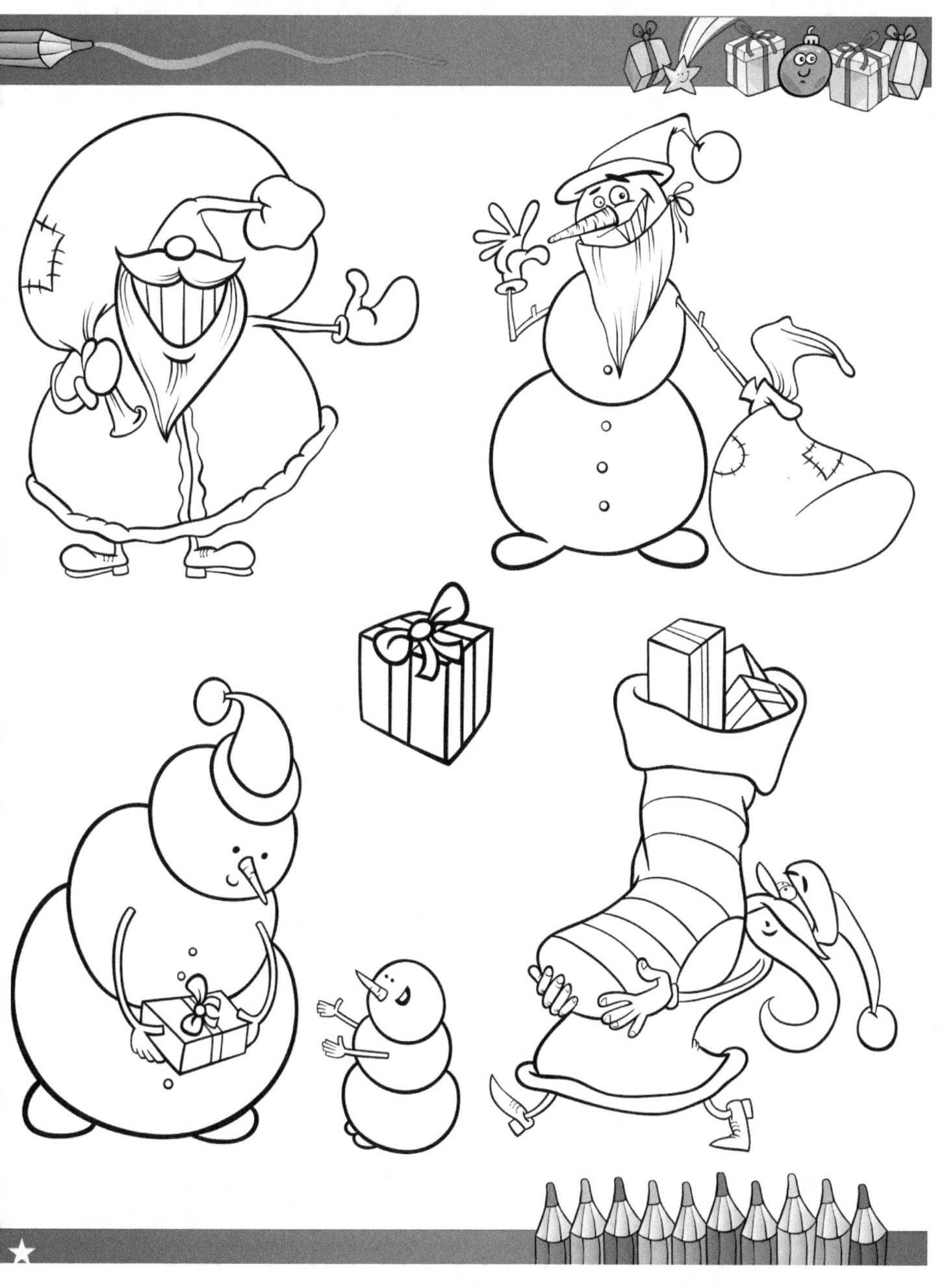

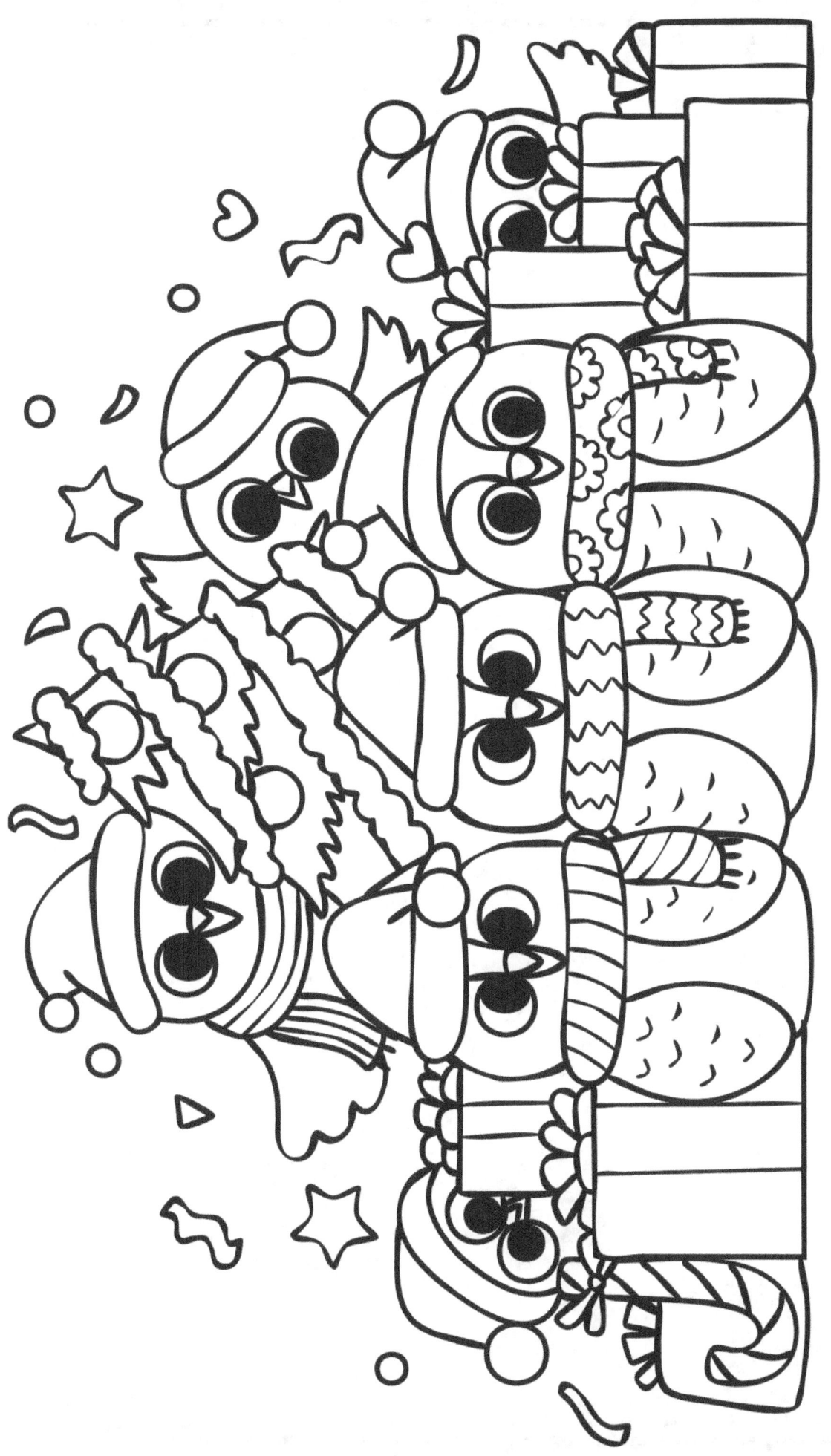

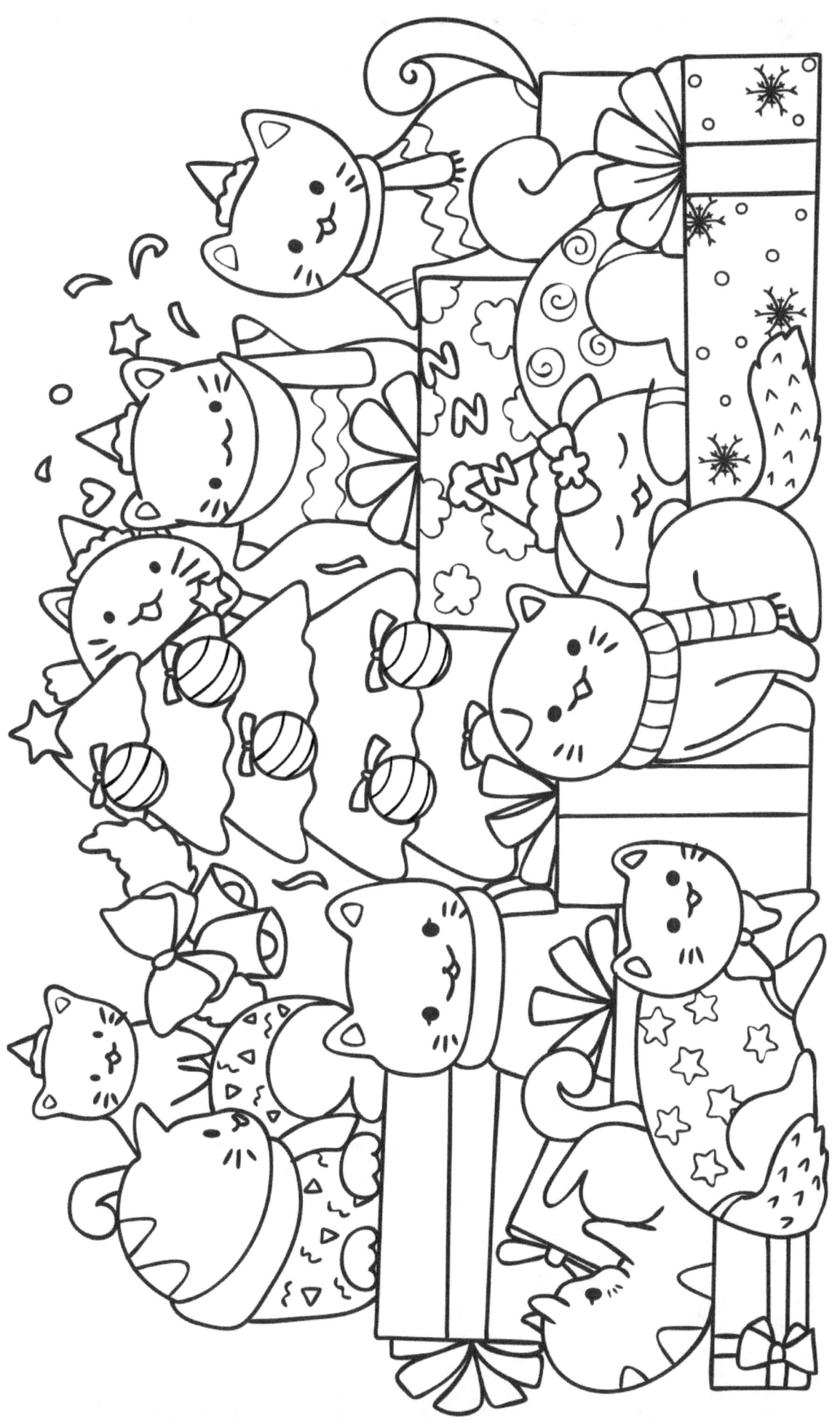

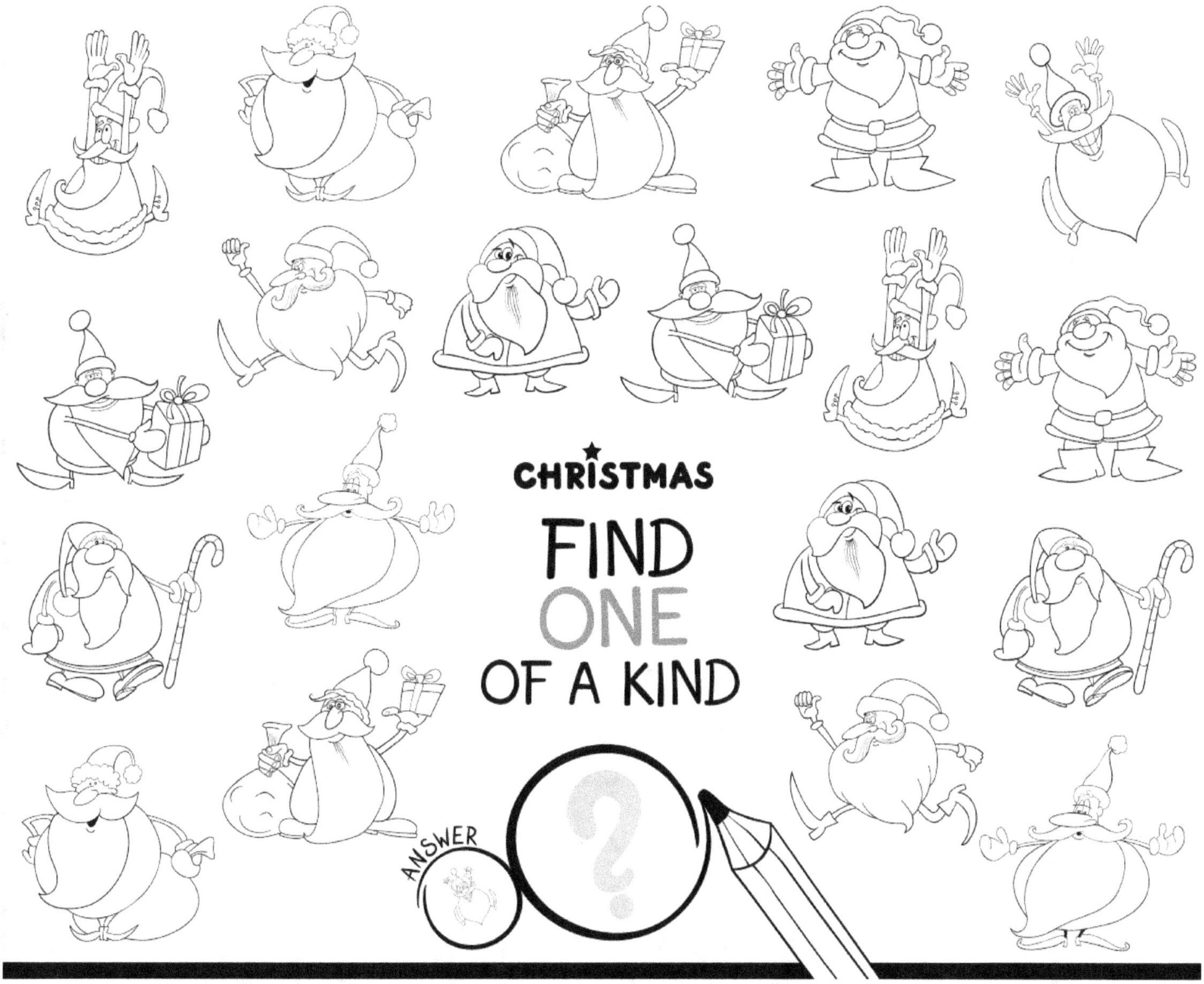

CHRISTMAS

FIND
ONE
OF A KIND

ANSWER

?

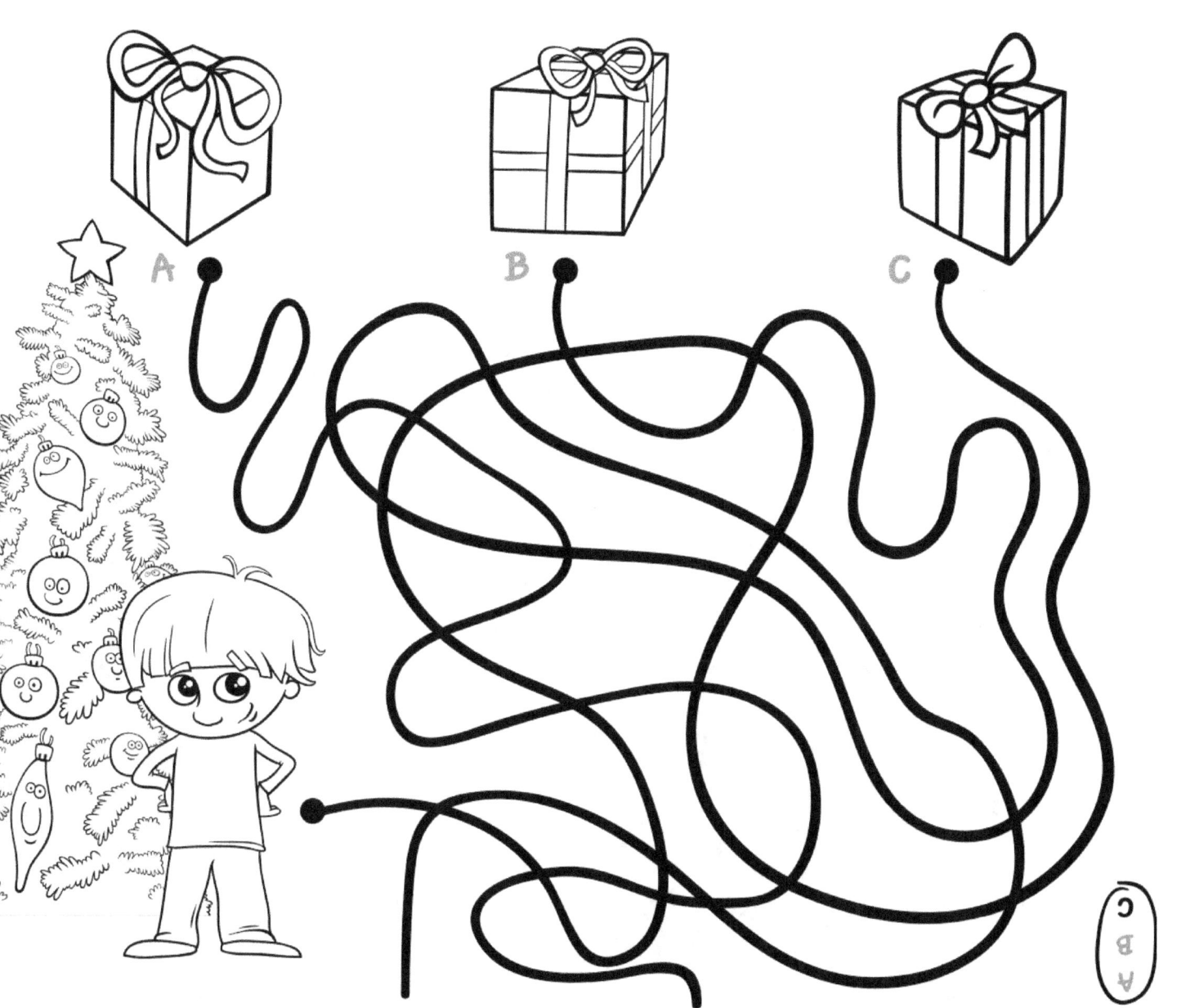

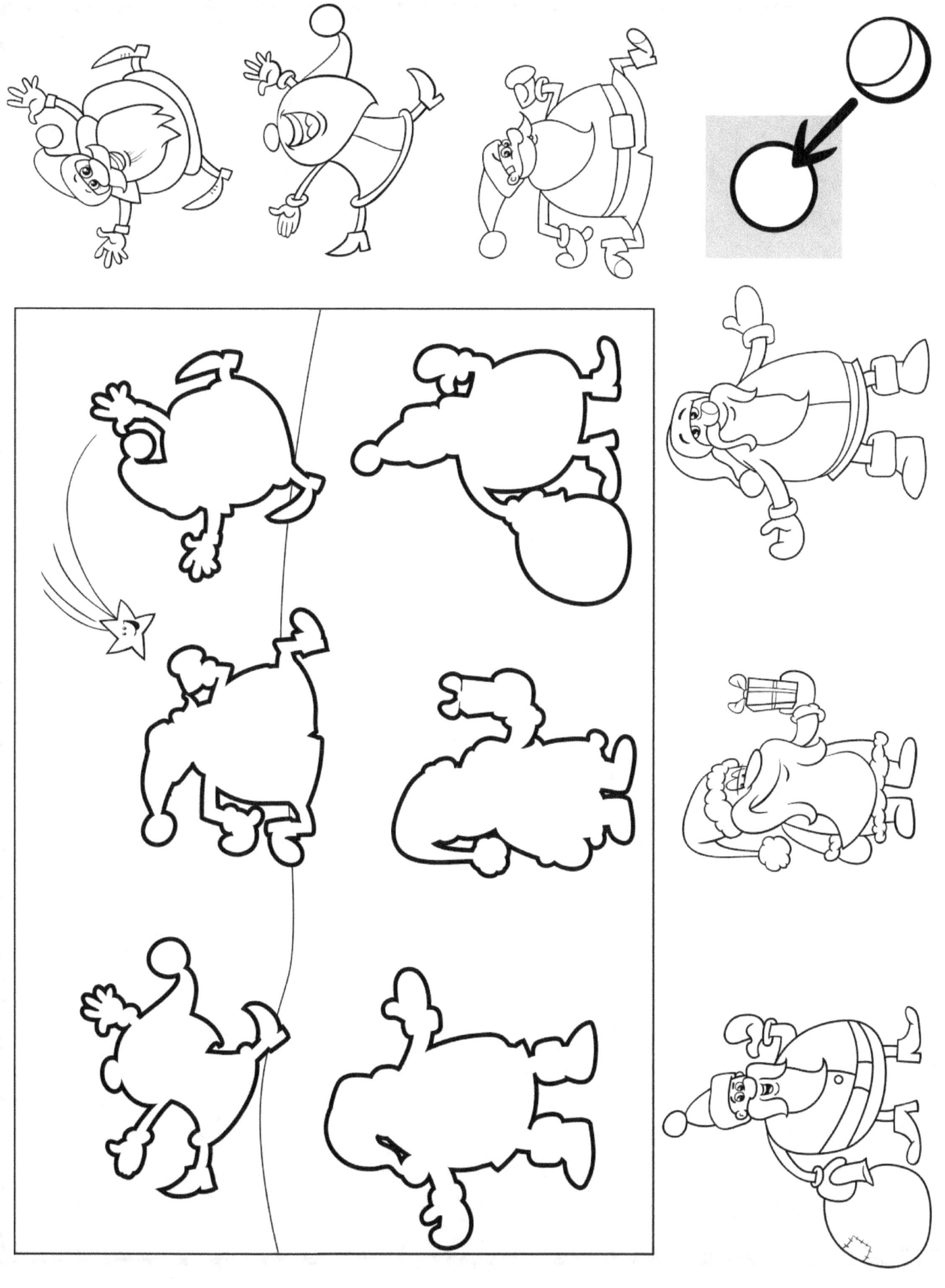

WHAT COMES NEXT?

1

2

3

4

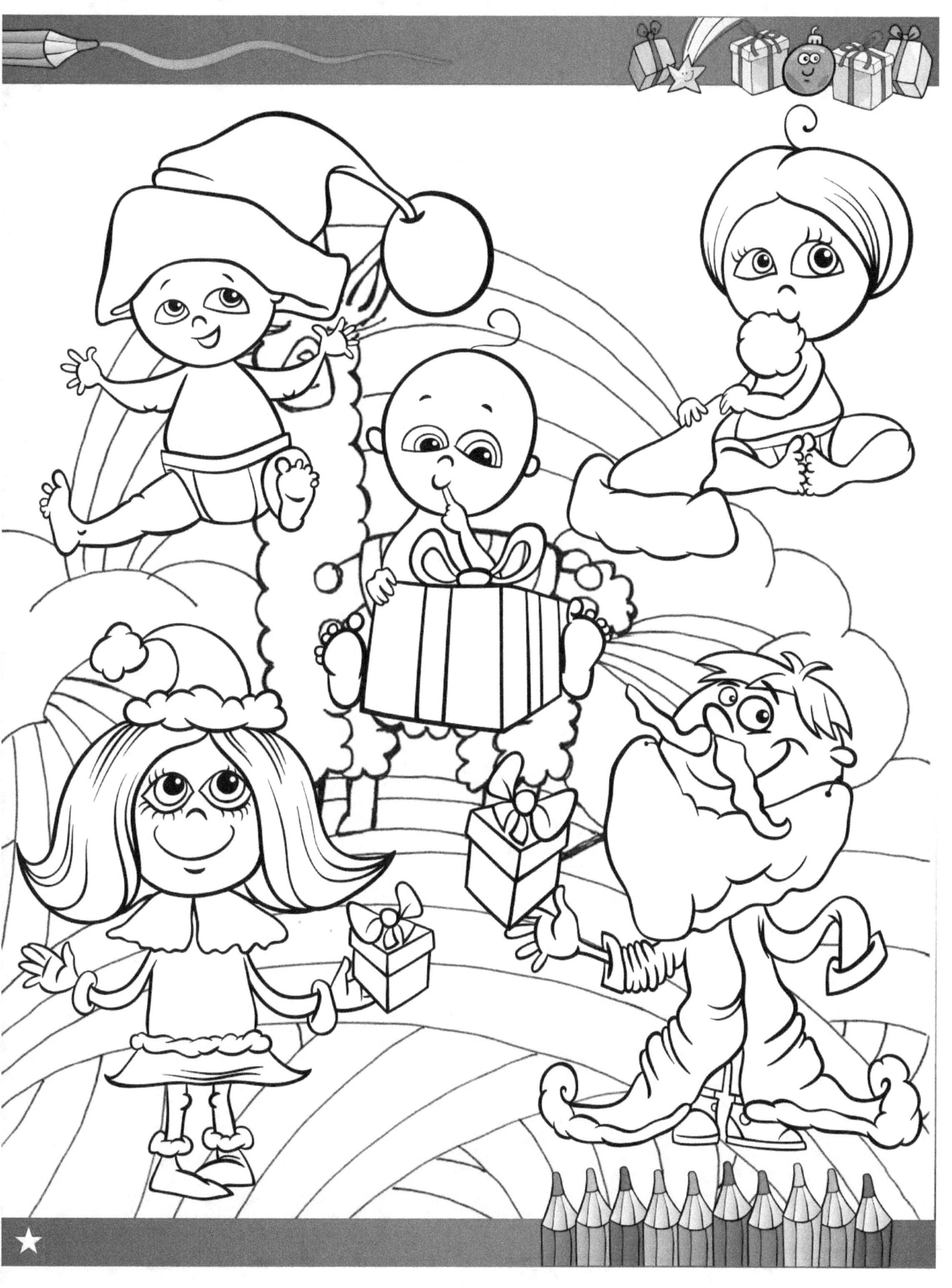

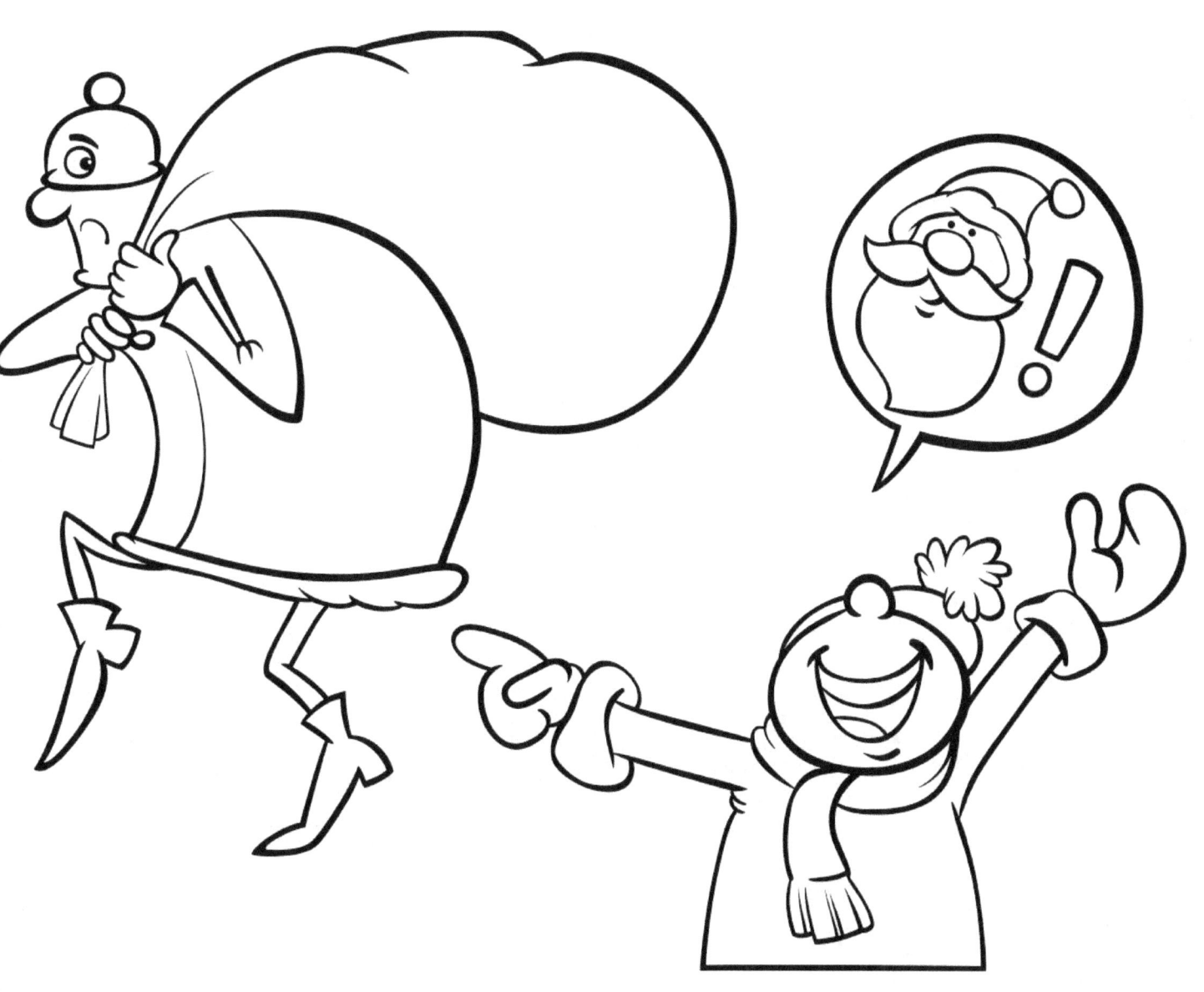

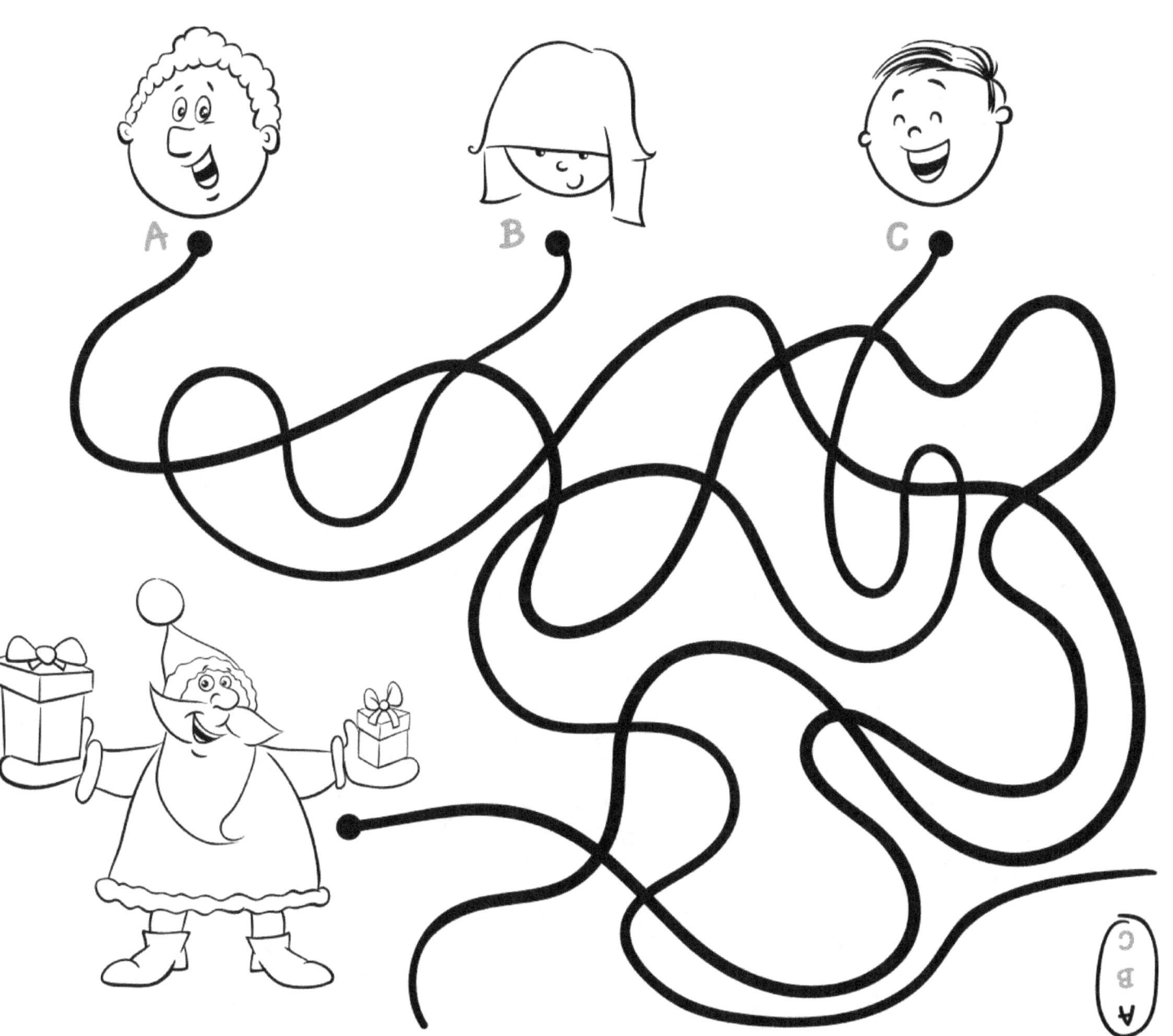

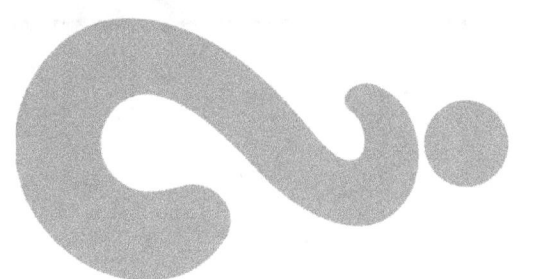
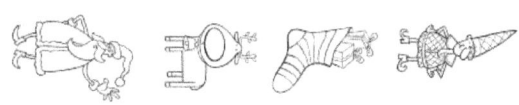

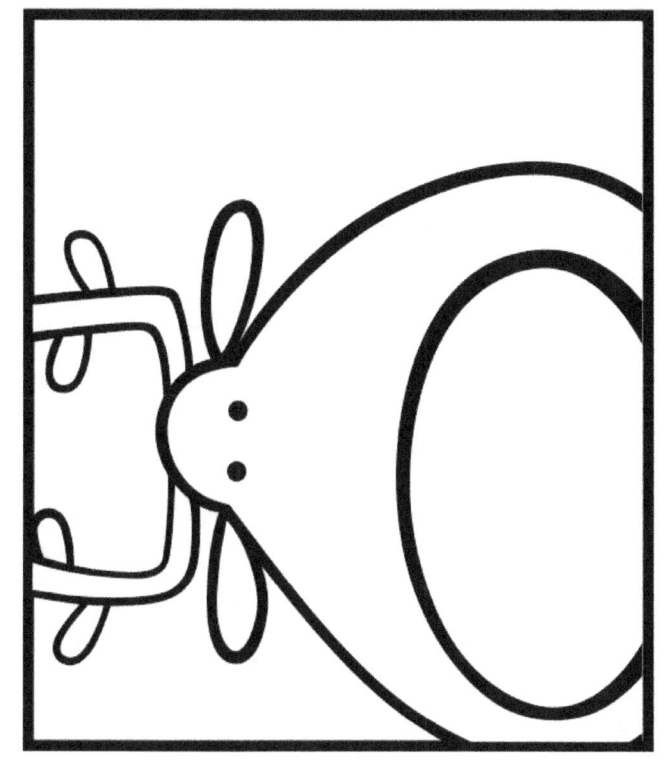
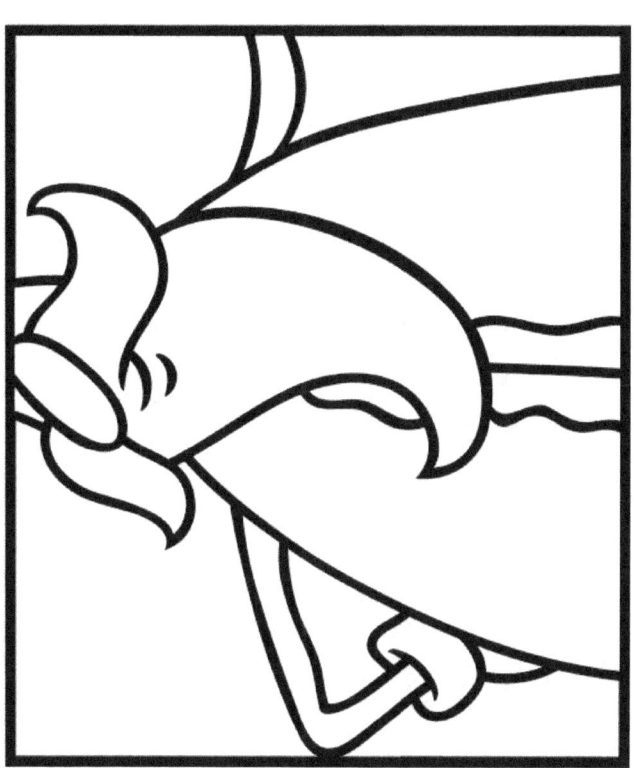

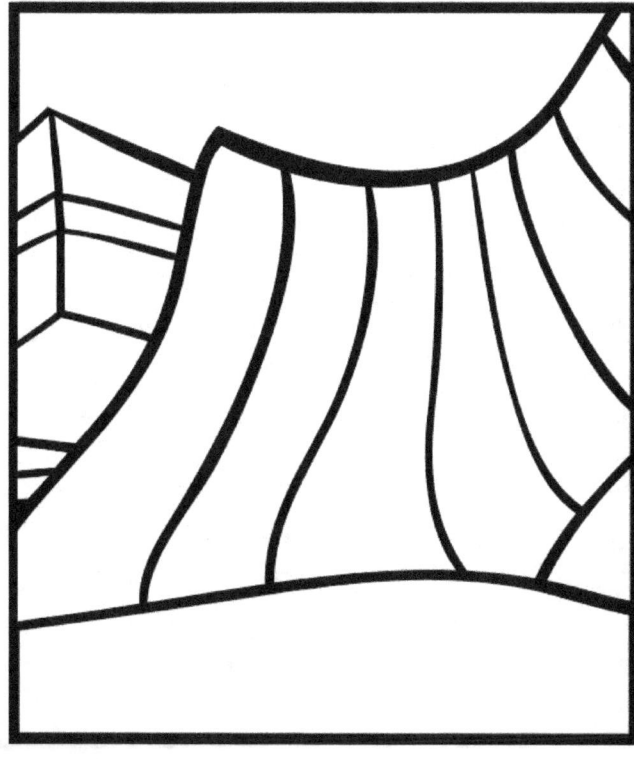
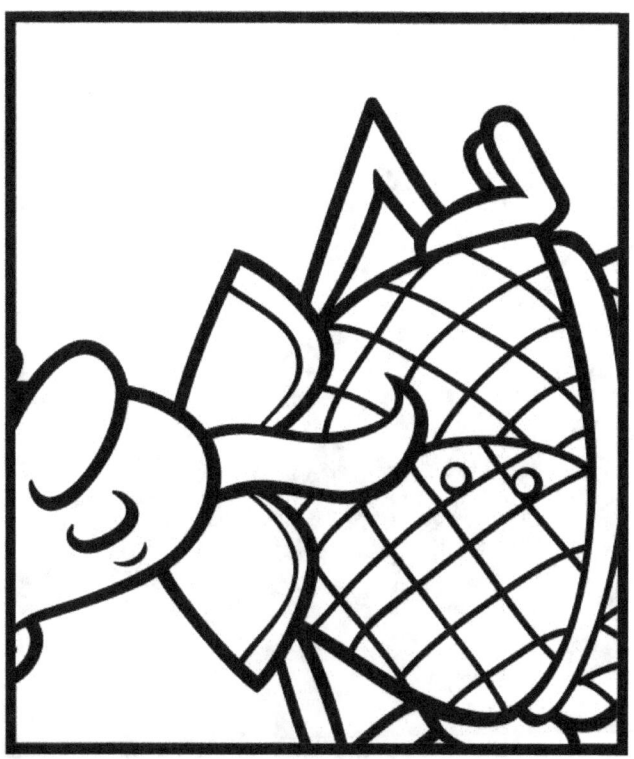

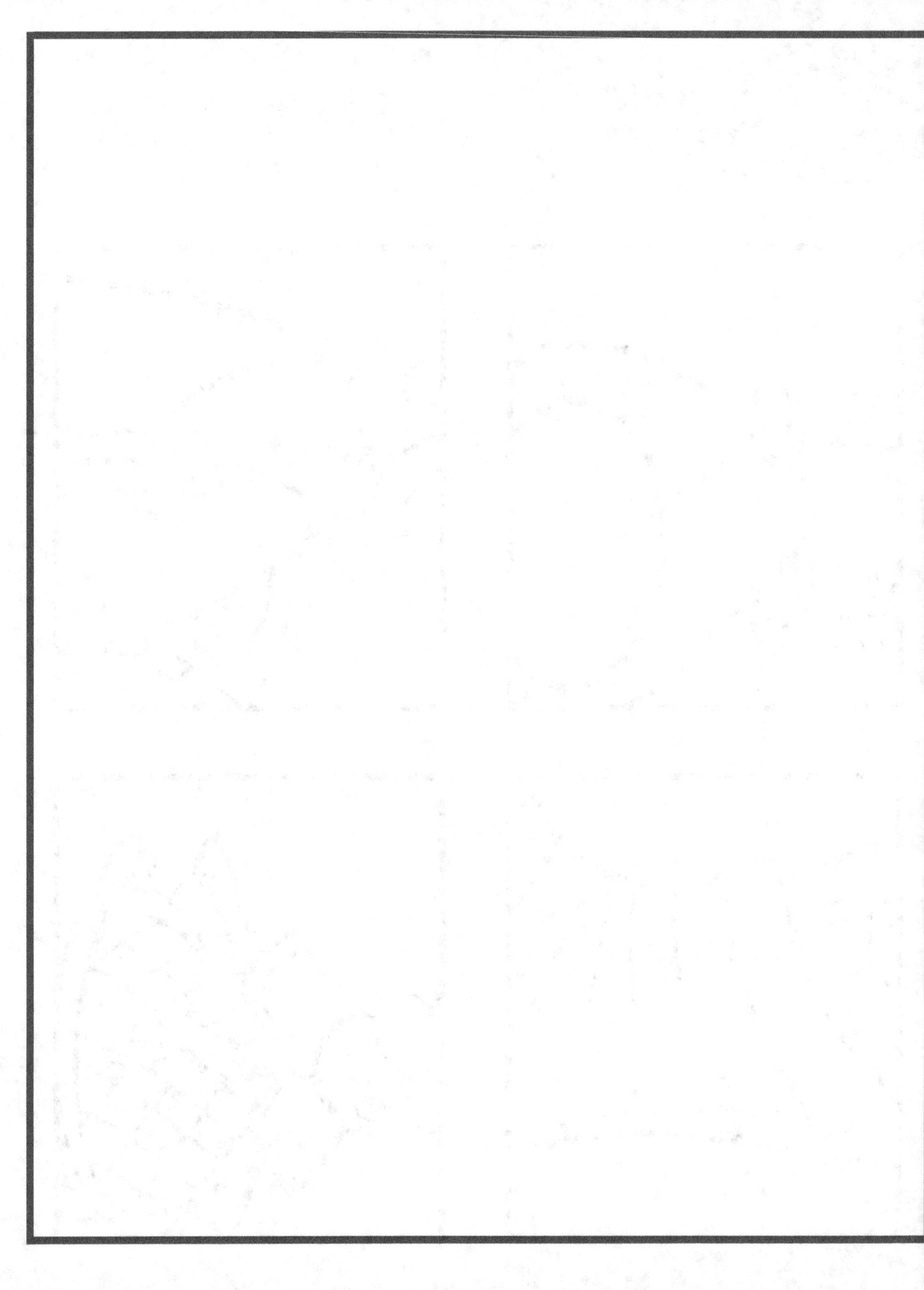

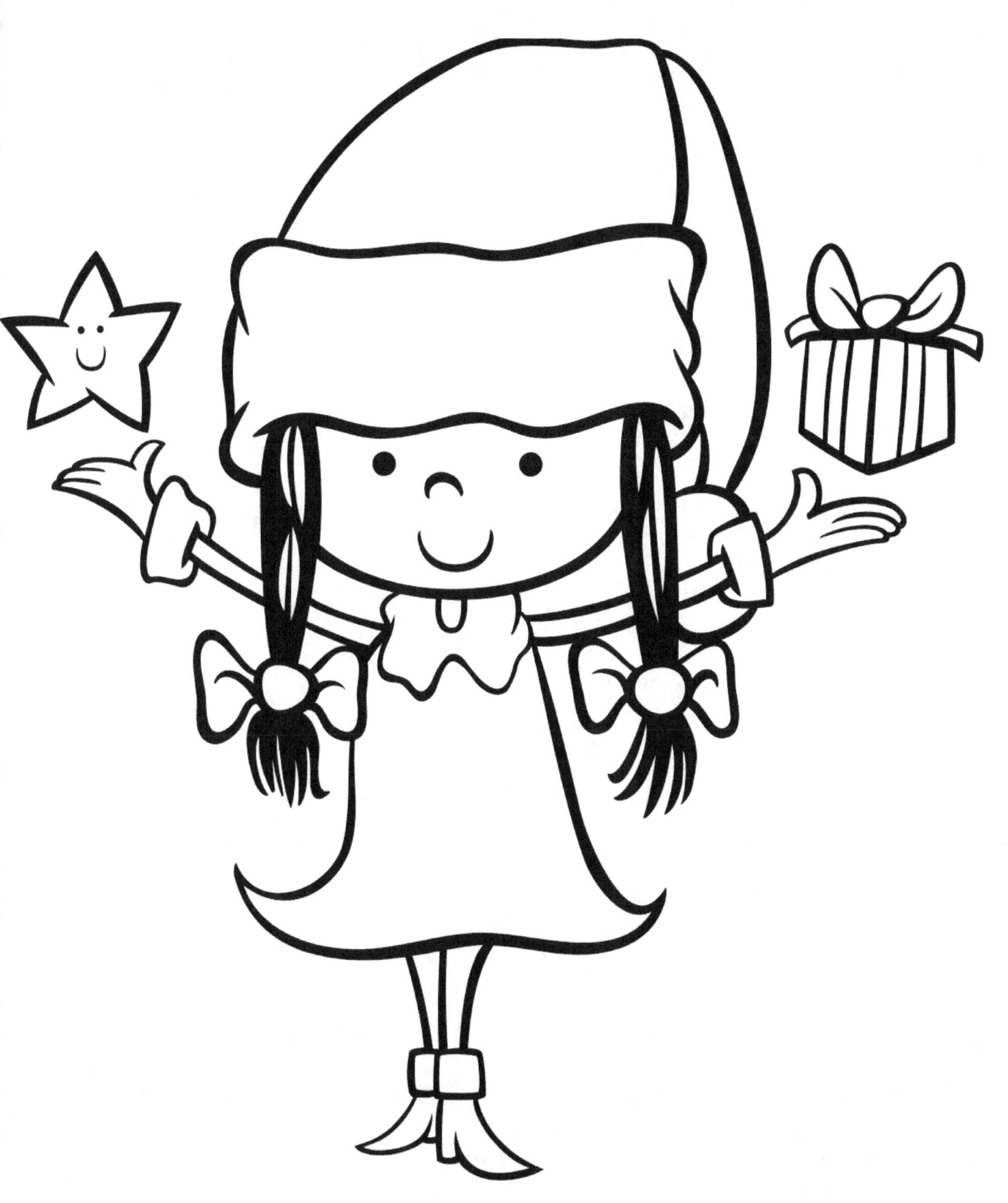

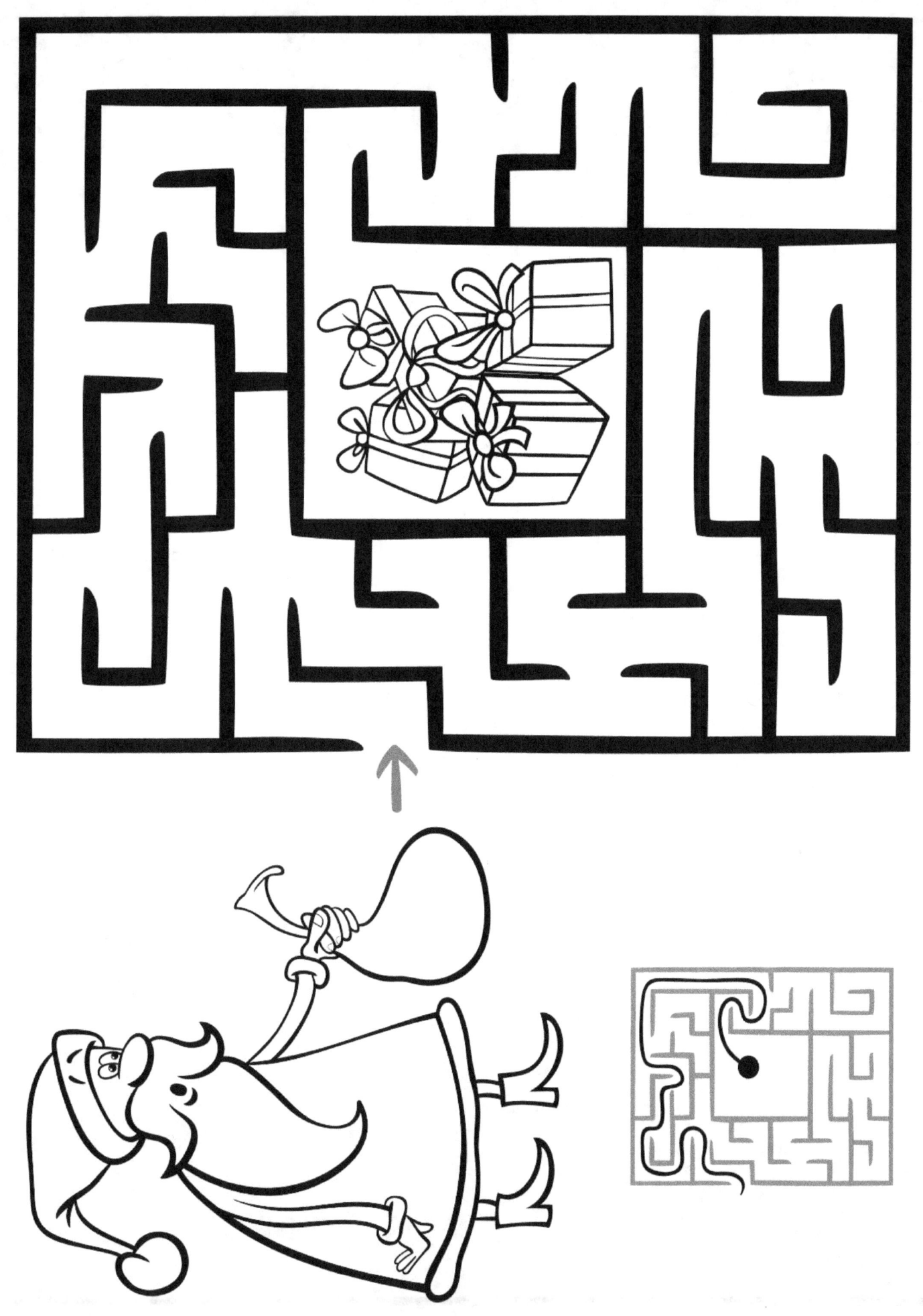

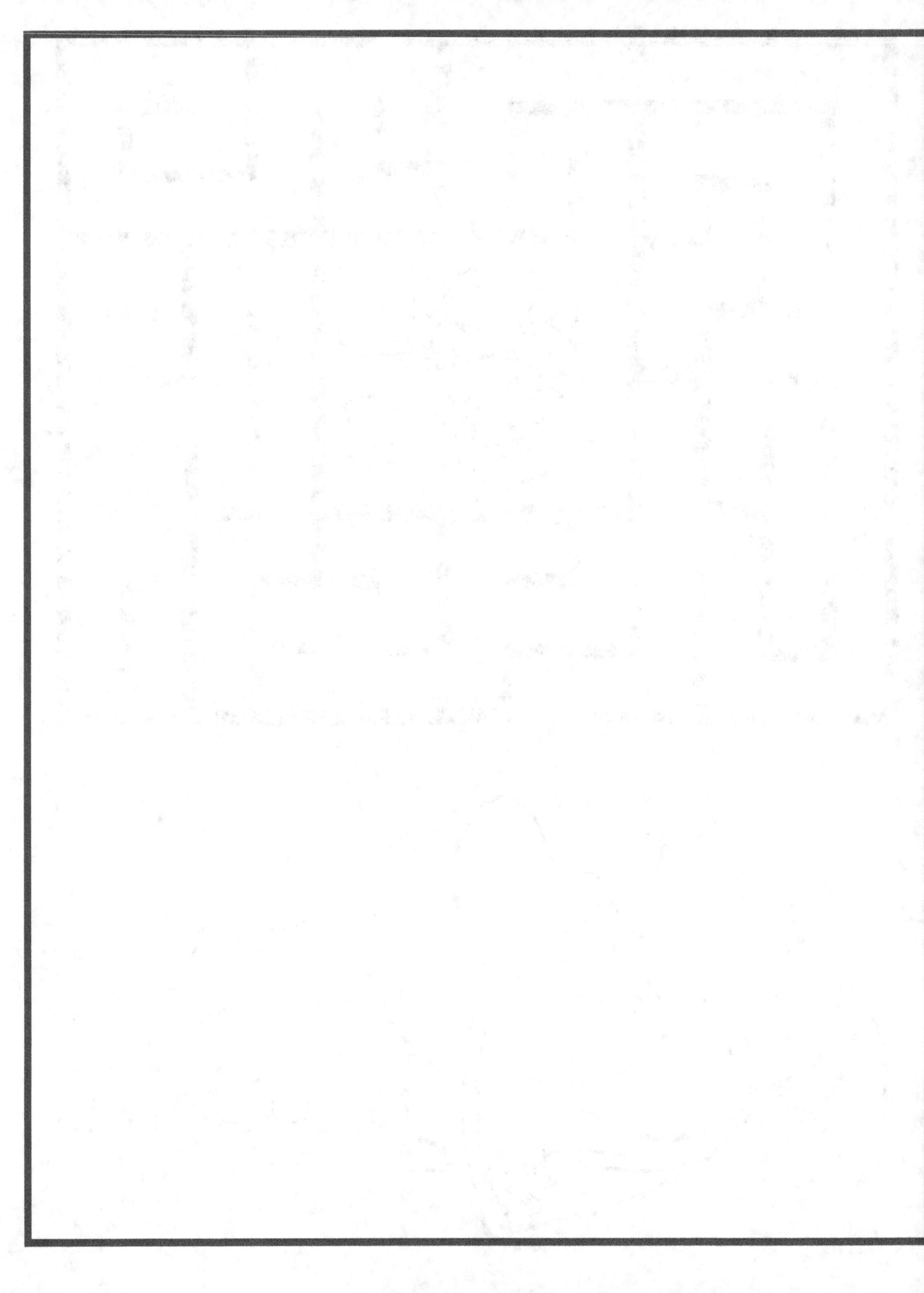

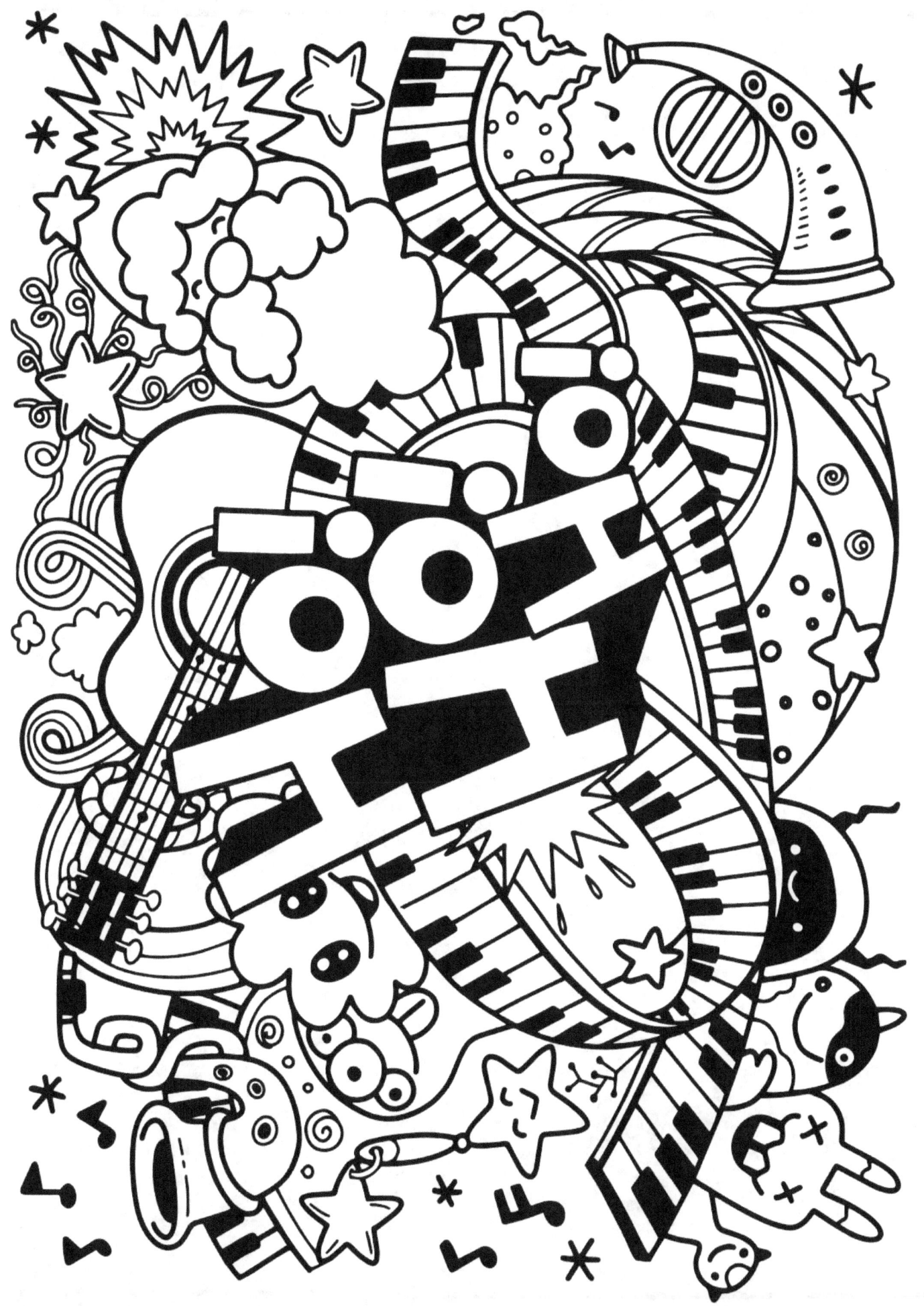

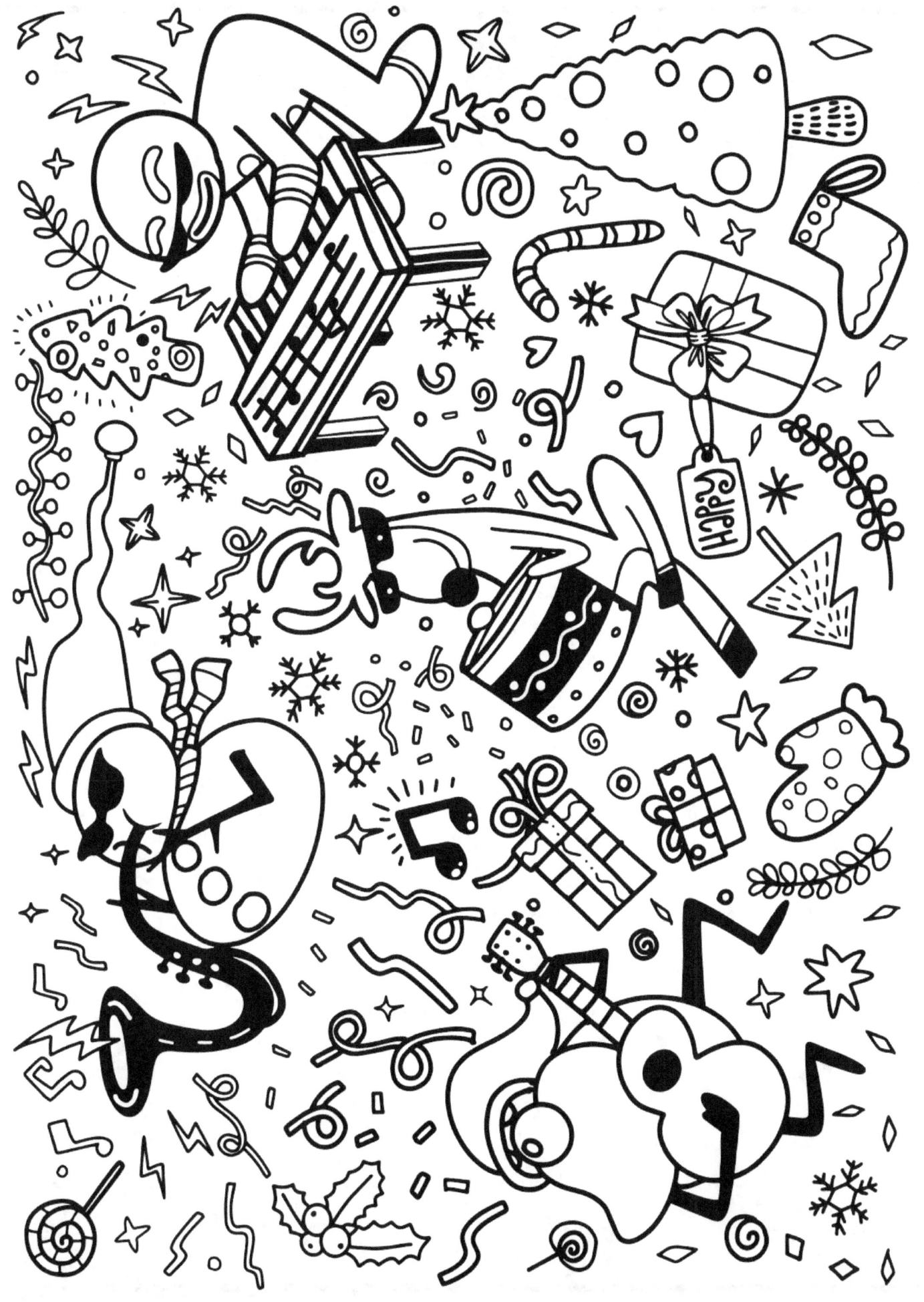

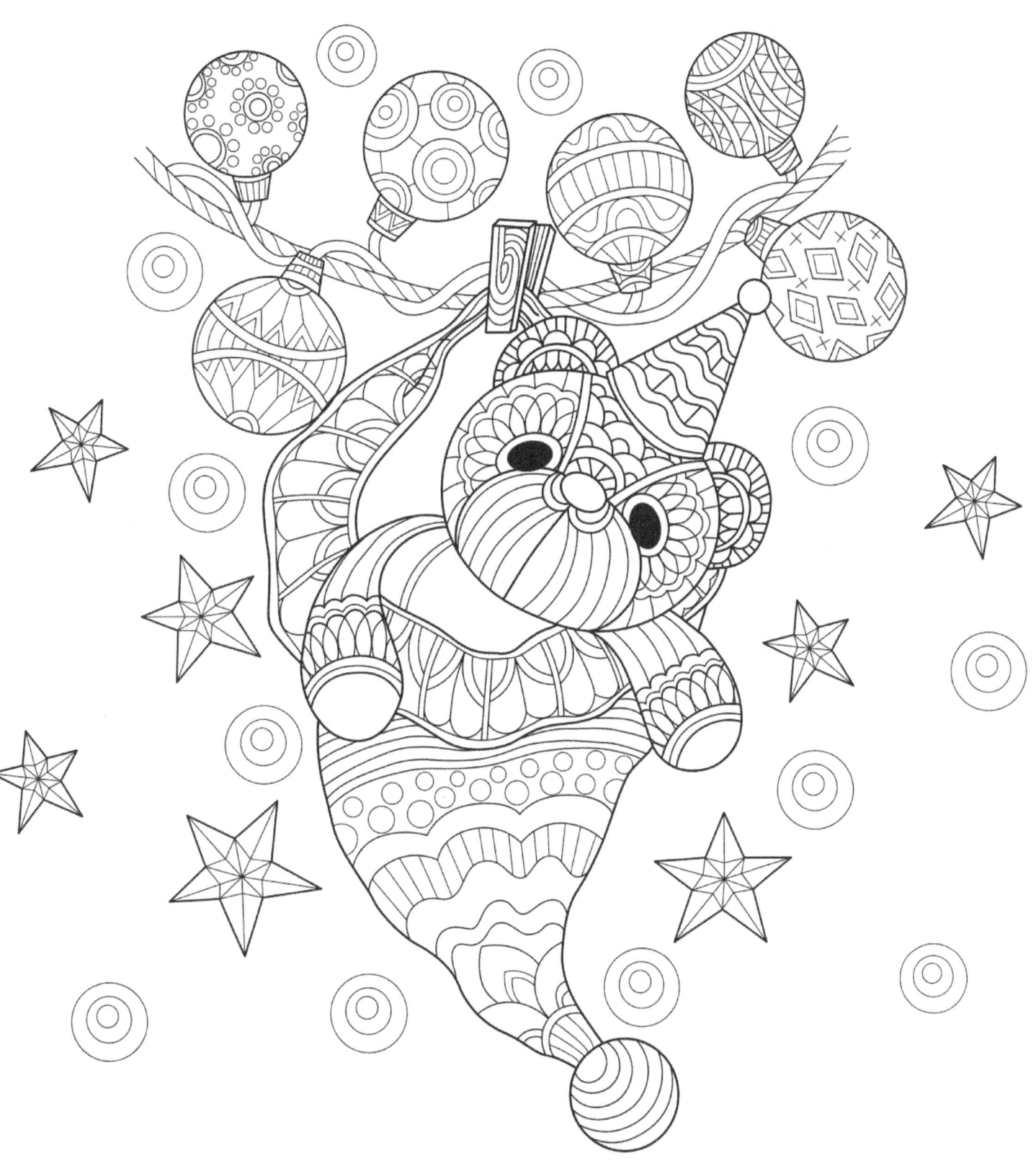

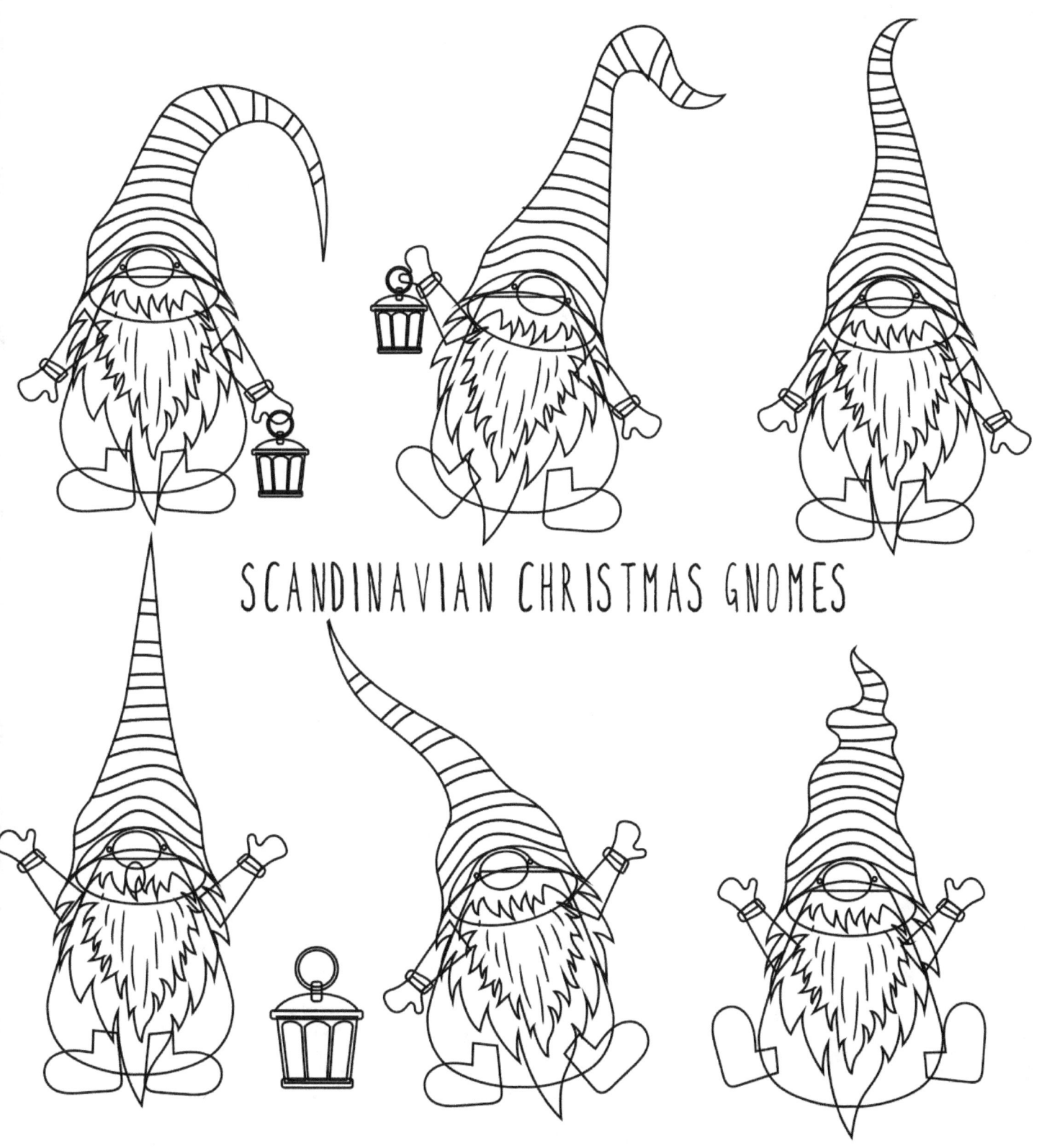

SCANDINAVIAN CHRISTMAS GNOMES